ASTRAL ANOMALY

To the fire, big or small, in your heart that inspires you to rise every day.

~

~

Lulu Publishing

627 Davis Dr #300

Morrisville, NC 27560

(919)-459-5858

www.lulu.com

~

ISBN: 978-1-387-93108-8

"War, he sung, is toil and trouble; Honour but an empty bubble. Never ending, still beginning, fighting still, and still destroying. If the world be worth thy winning, think, oh thing, it worth thy enjoying."

-John Dryden

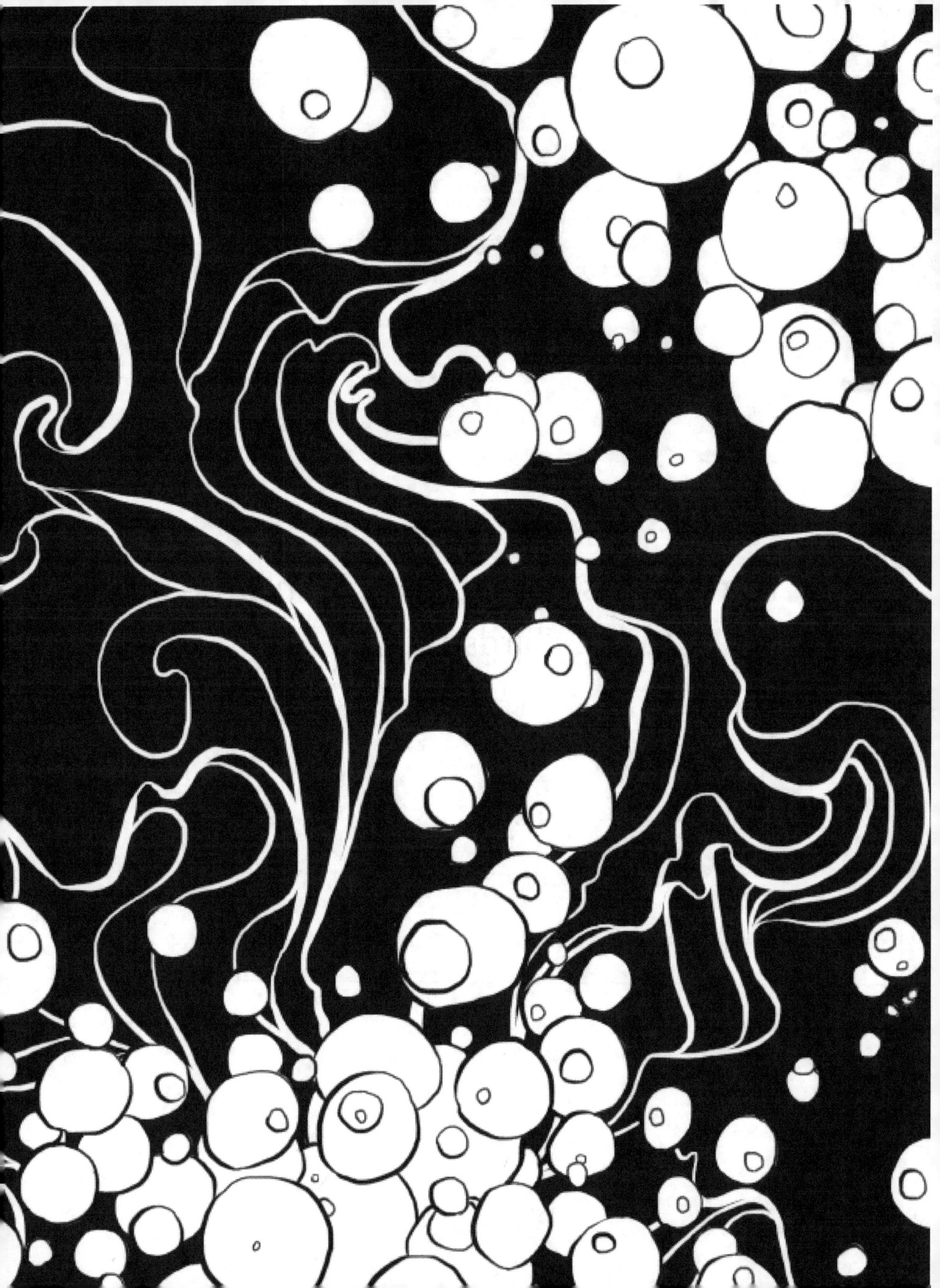

"The forest is a quiet place if only the best birds sing."

-Kay Johnson

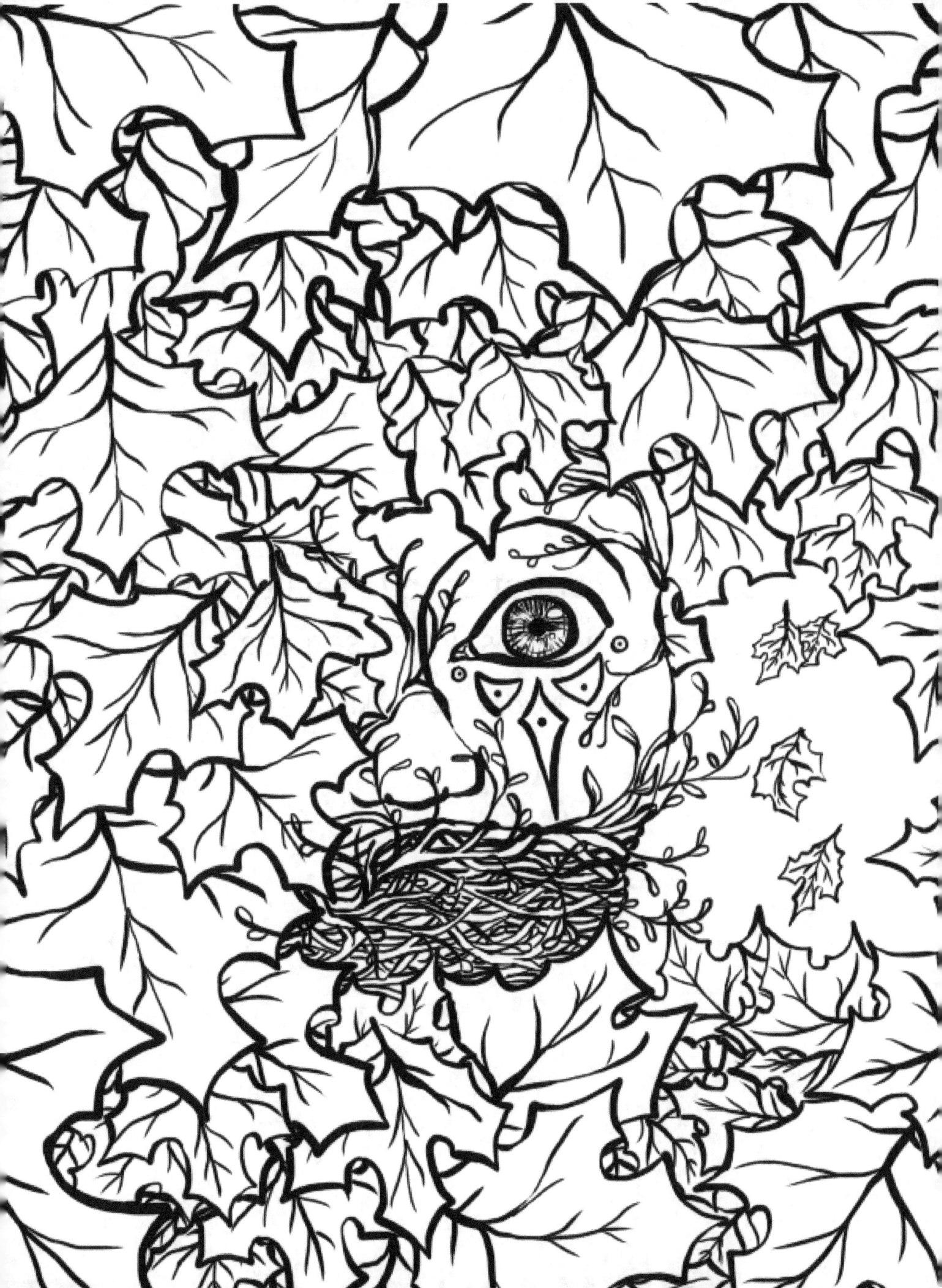

"Since we cannot change reality, let us change the eyes which see reality."

-Nikos Kazantzakis

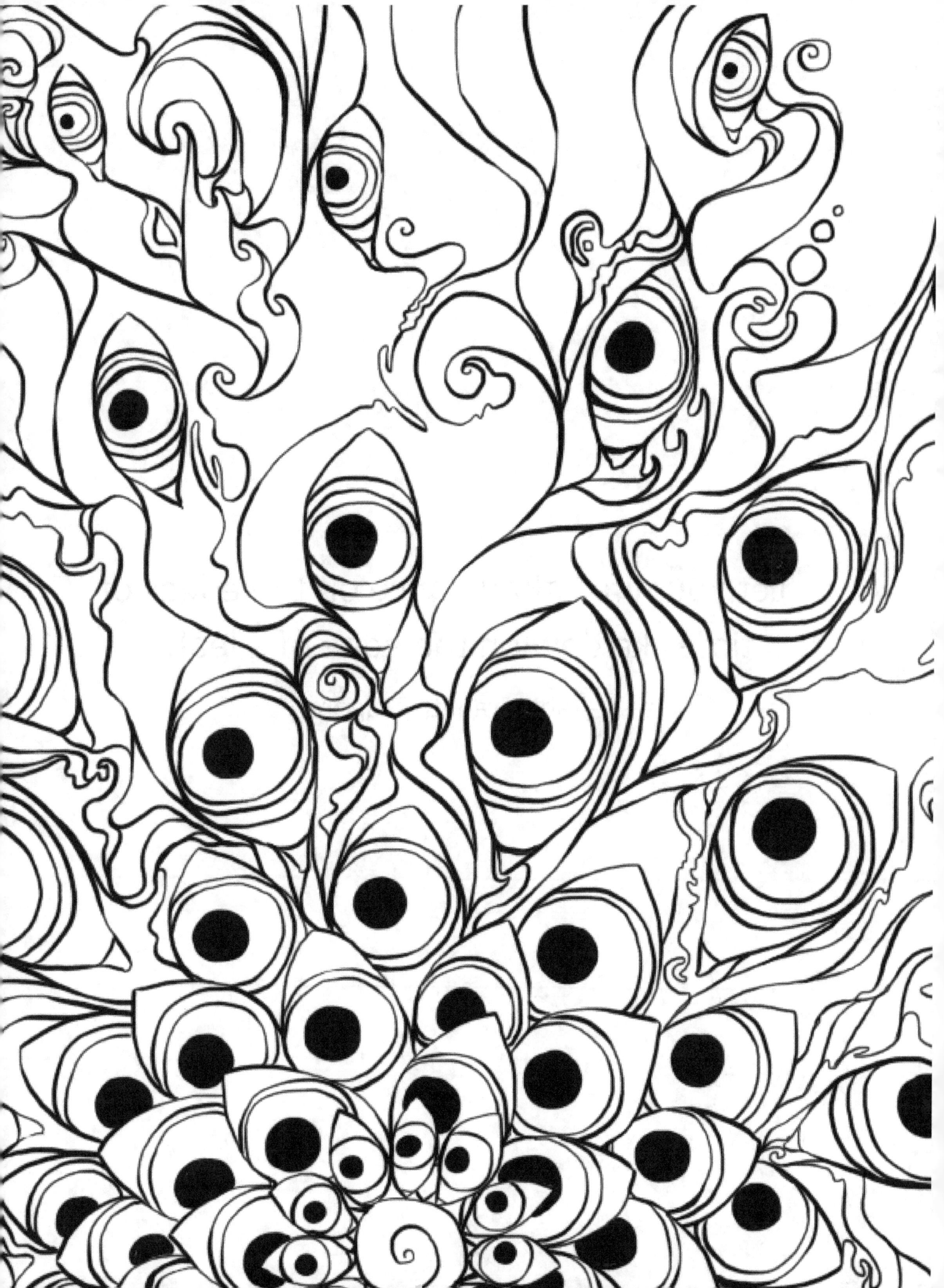

"Let your life lightly dance on the edges of time like dew on the edge of a leaf."

-Rabindranath Tragore

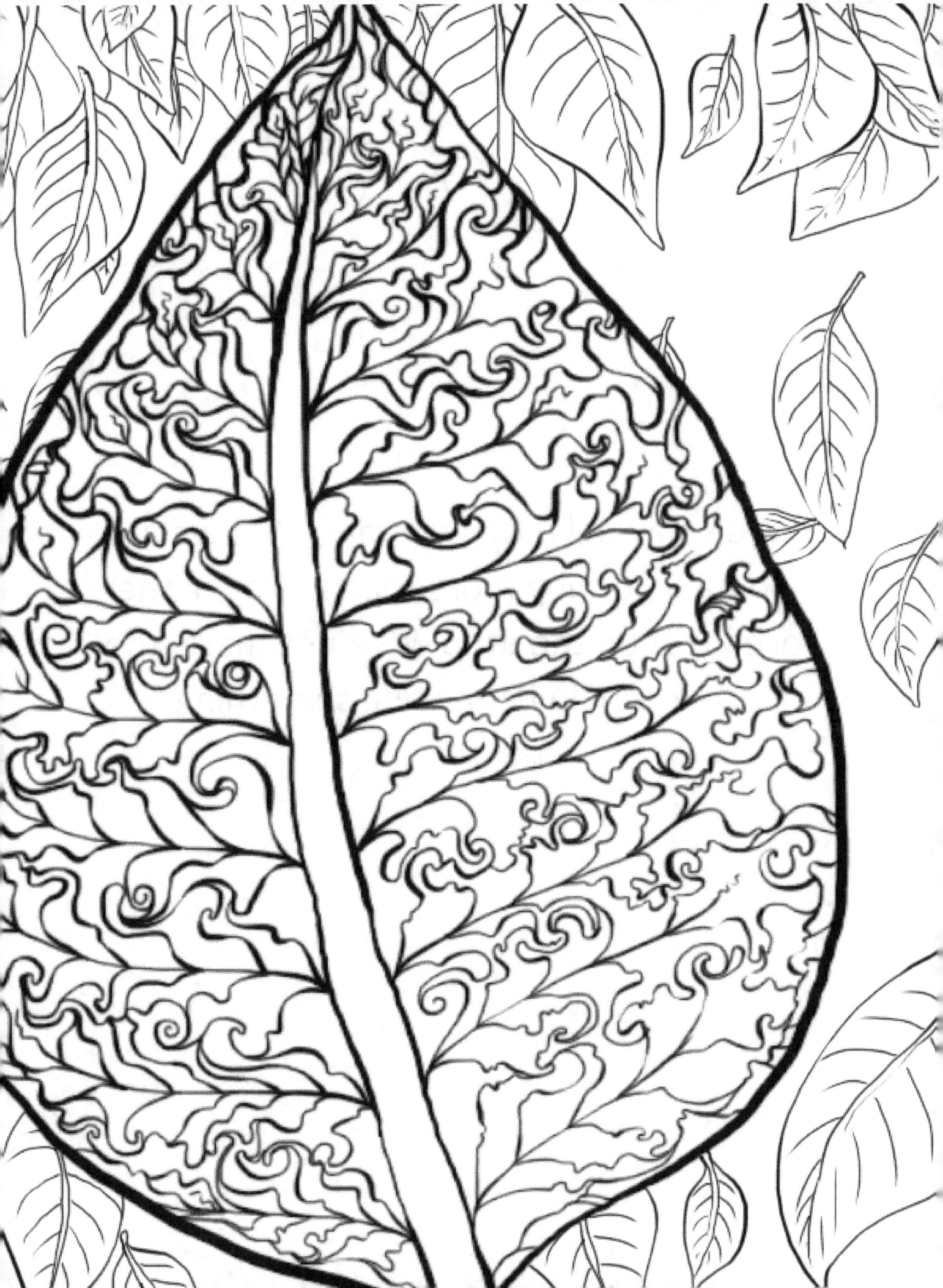

"We know only too well that what we are doing is nothing more than a drop in the ocean. But if the drop were not there, the ocean would be missing something."

-Mother Teresa

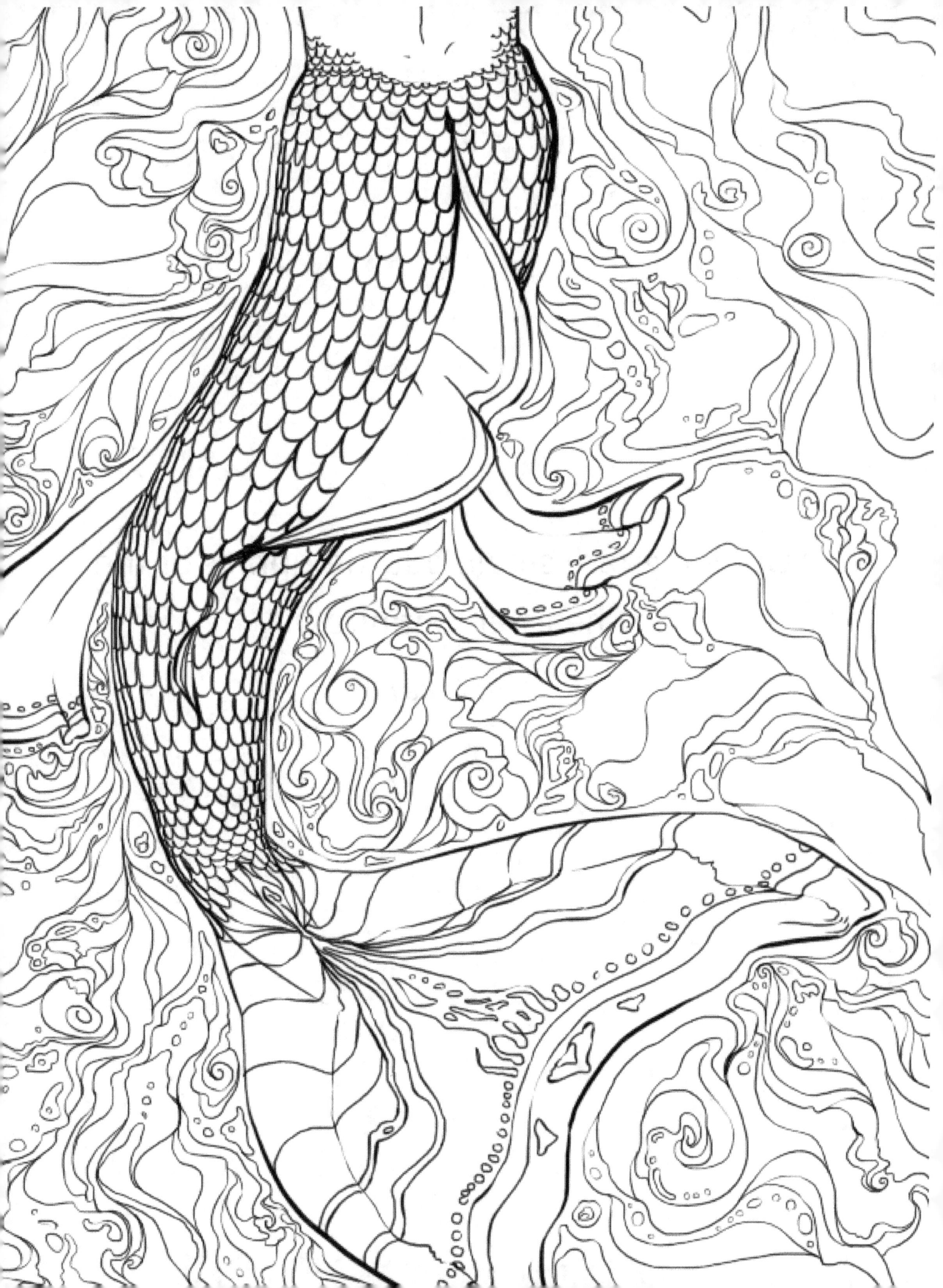

"Our wings are small, but the ripples of the heart are infinite."

-Amit Ray

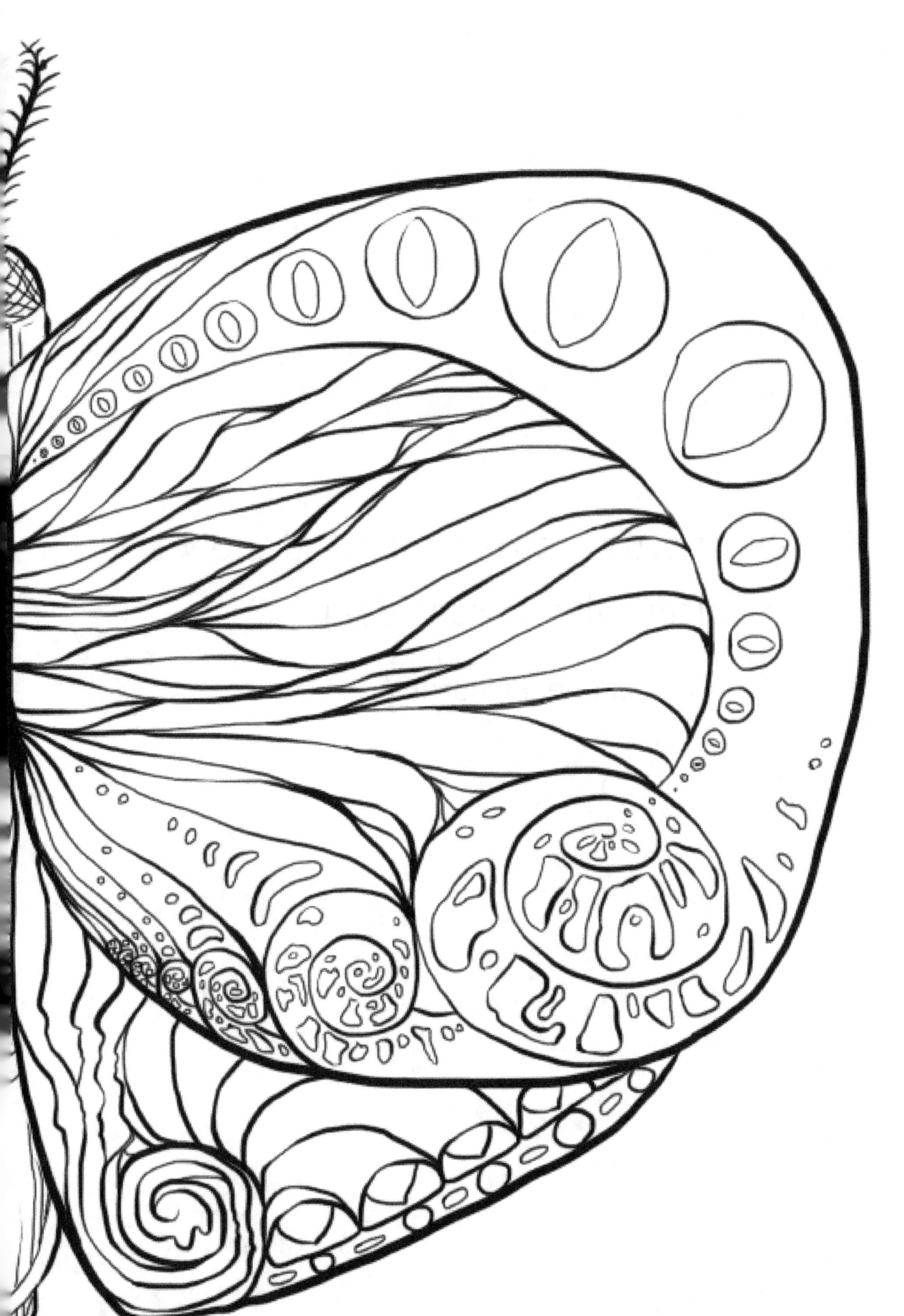

"Where words are restrained, the eyes often talk a great deal."

-Samuel Richardson

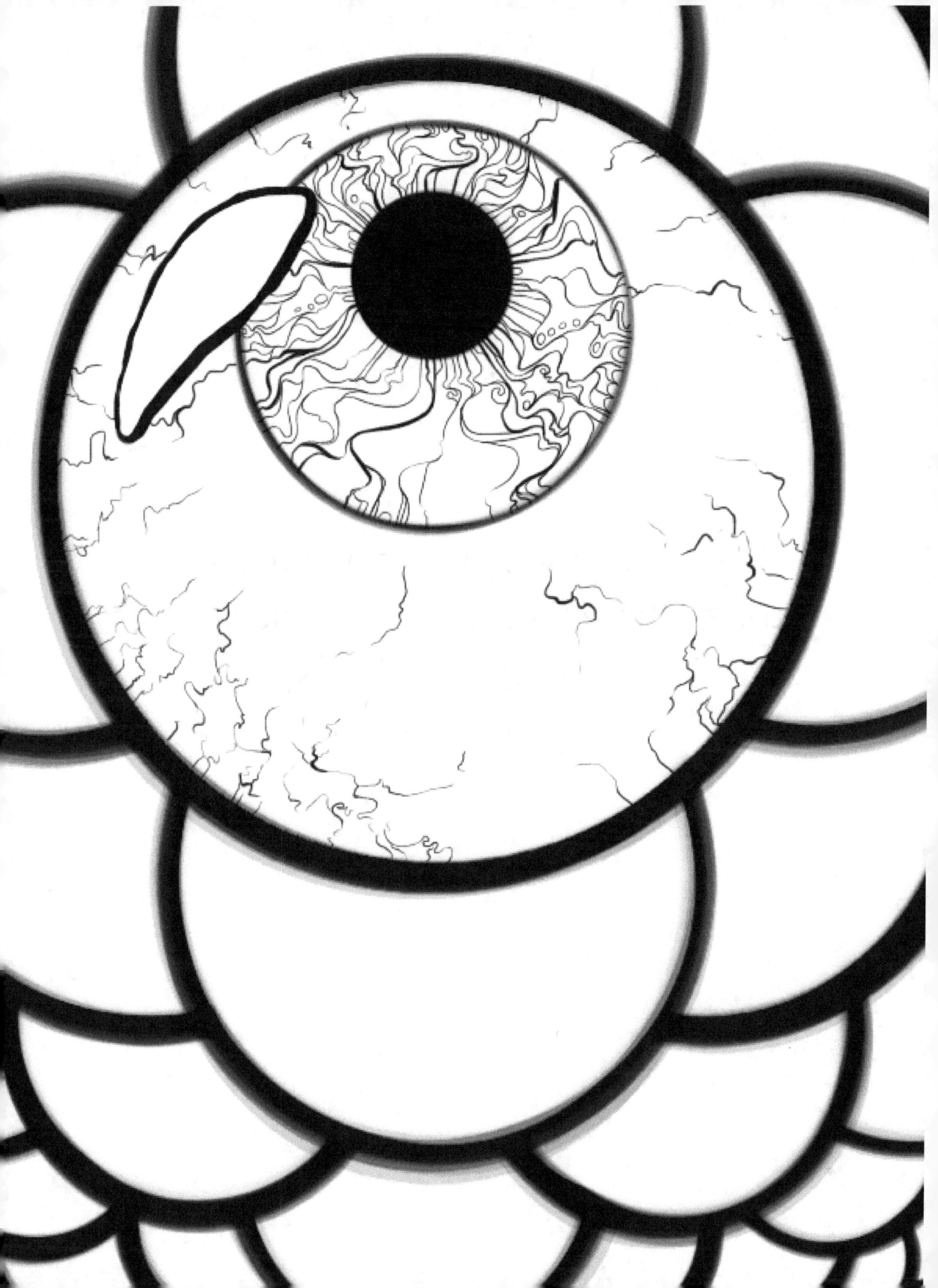

"There is geometry in the humming of the strings, there is music in the spacing of the spheres."

-Pythagoras

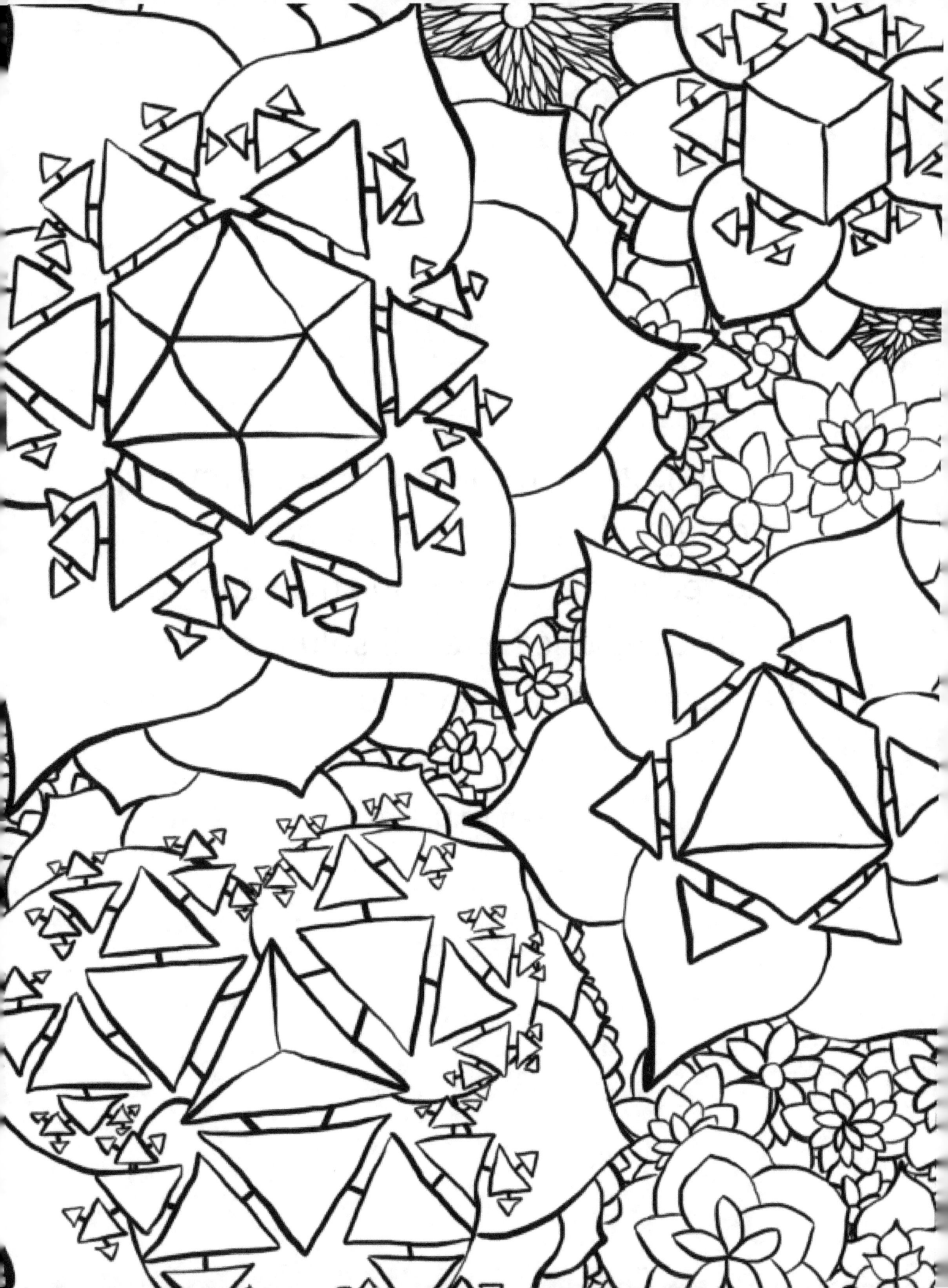

"Crystals grew inside rock like arithmetic flowers. They lengthened and spread, added plane to plane in an awed and perfect obedience to an absolute geometry that even stones - maybe only the stones - understood.

-Annie Dillard

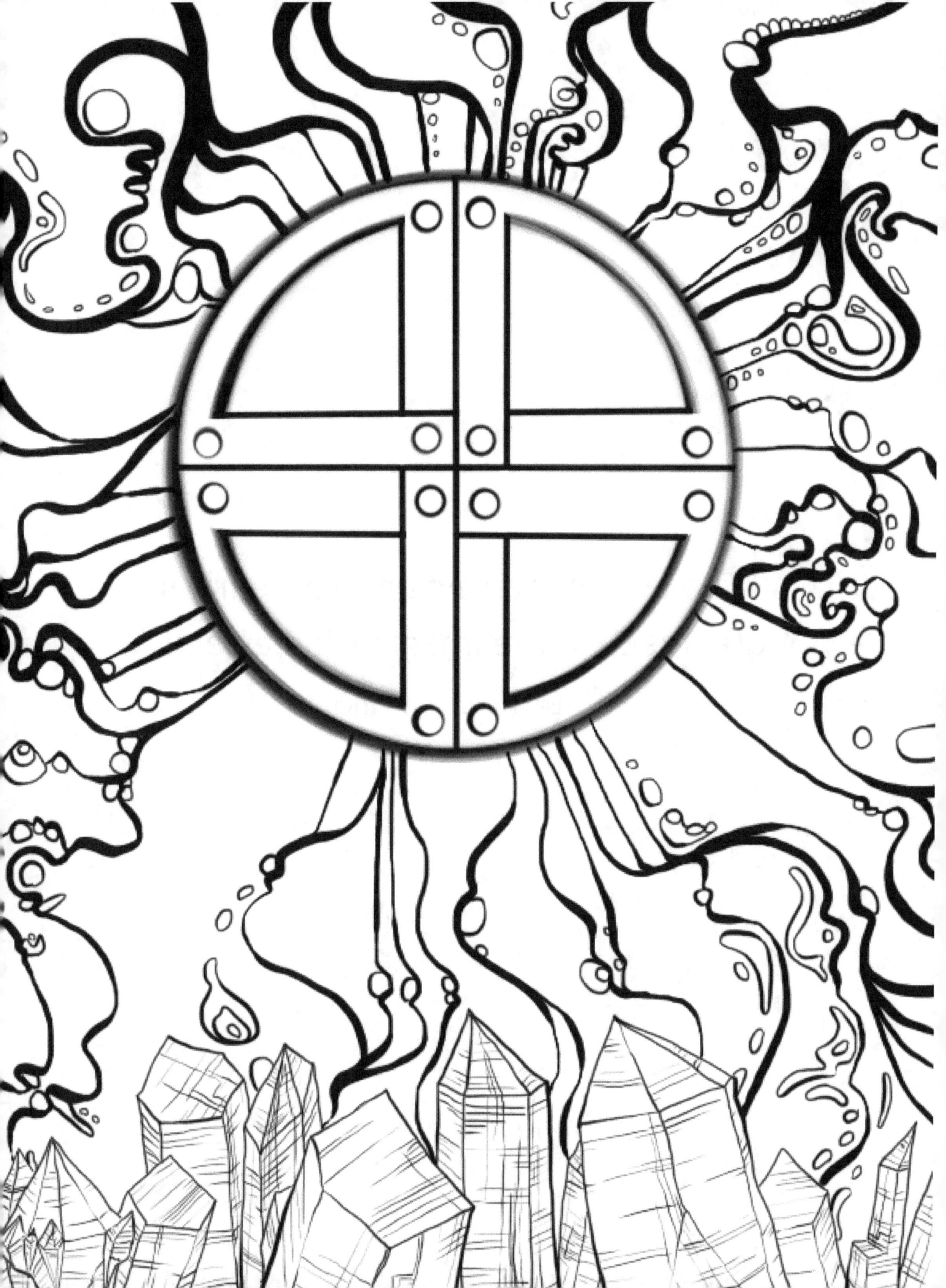

"The eye sees a thing more clearly in dreams than the imagination awake."

-Leonardo da Vinci

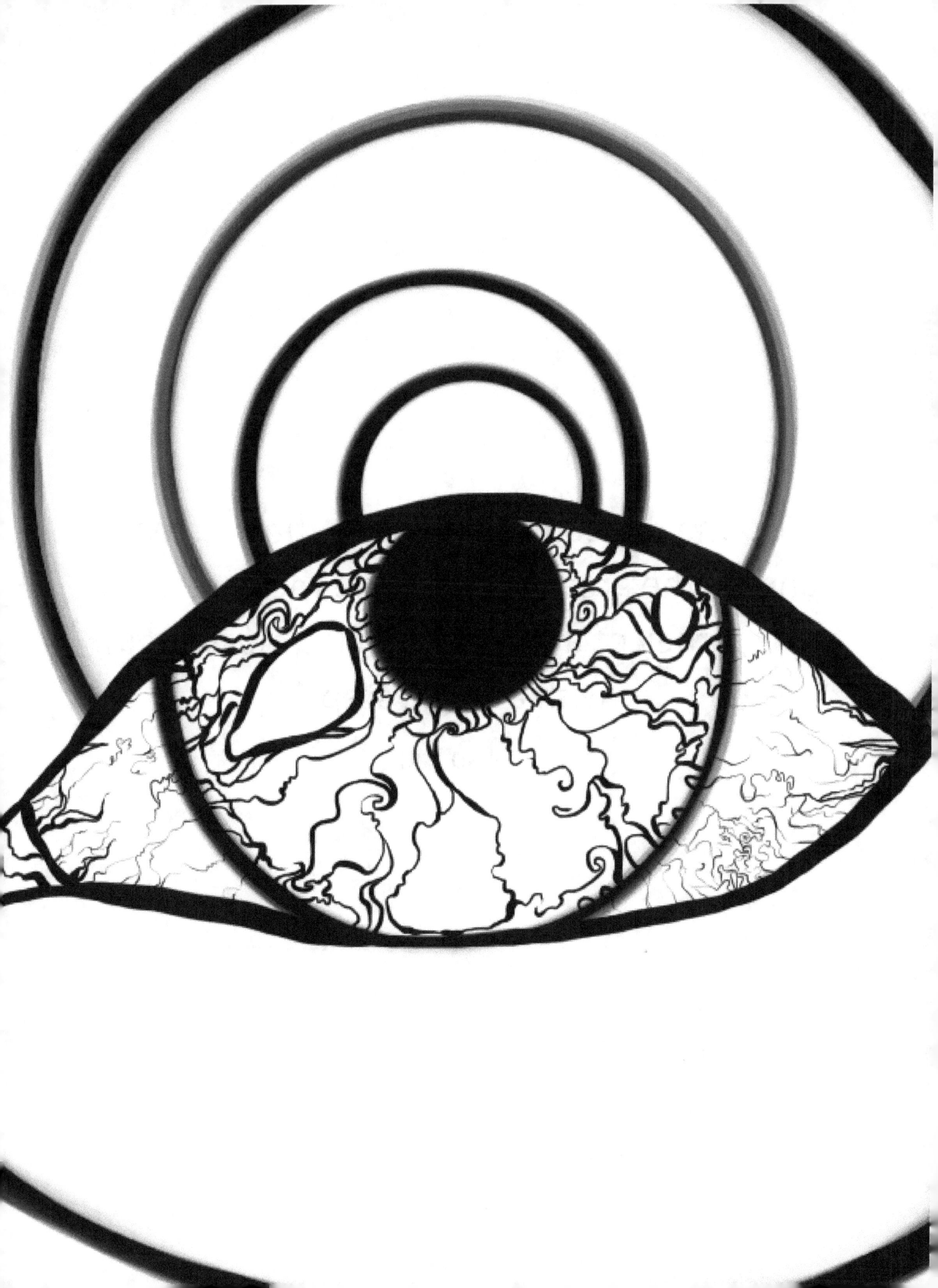

"Do the difficult things while they are easy and do the great things while they are small. A journey of a thousand miles must begin with a single step."

-Lao Tzu

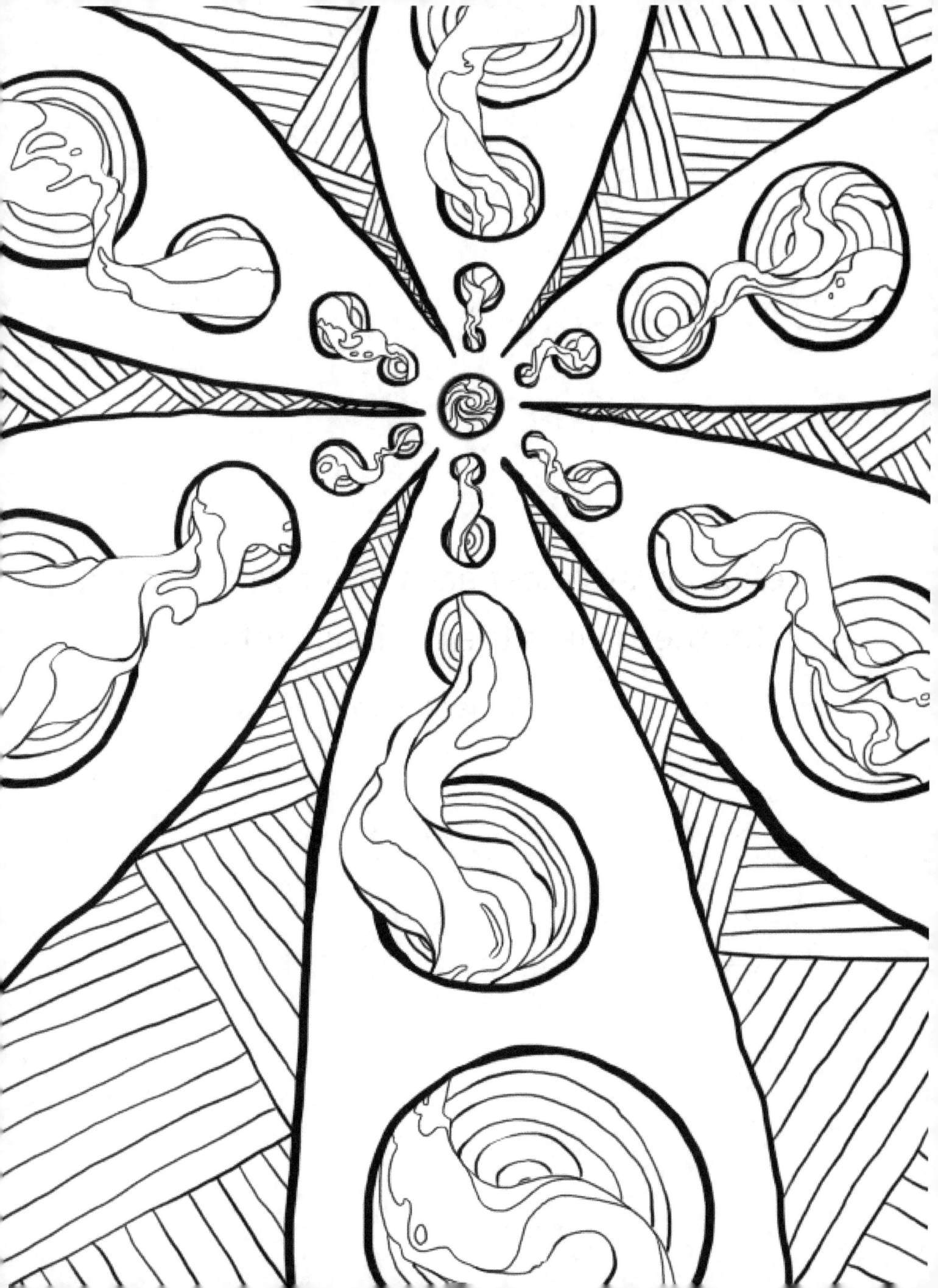

"Let us always meet each other with a smile, for the smile is the beginning of love."

-Mother Teresa

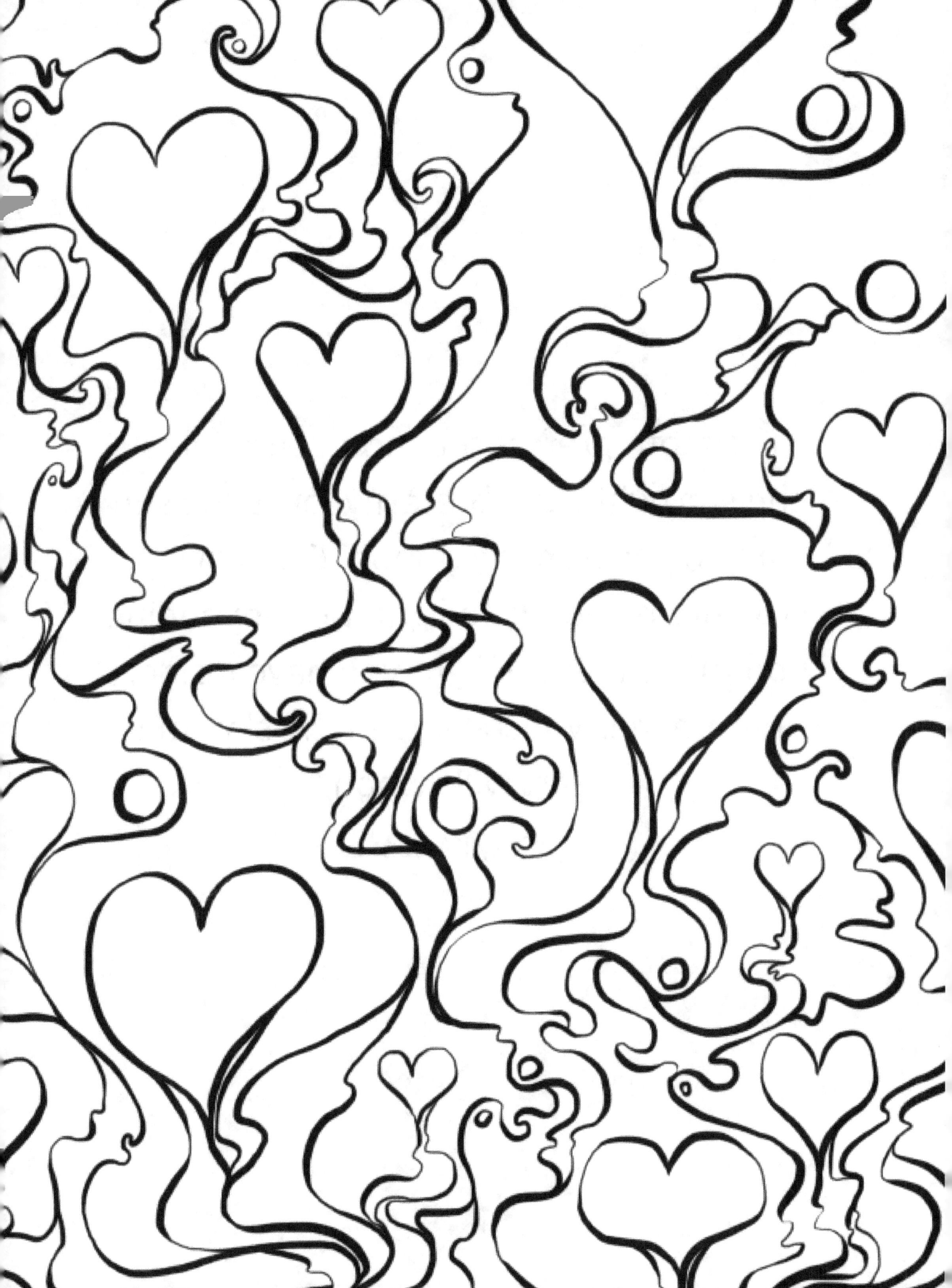

"The moth prefers the moon and detests the sun, while the butterfly loves the sun and hides from the moon. Every living creature responds to light. But depending on the amount of light you have inside, determines which lamp in the sky your heart will swoon."

-Suzy Kassem

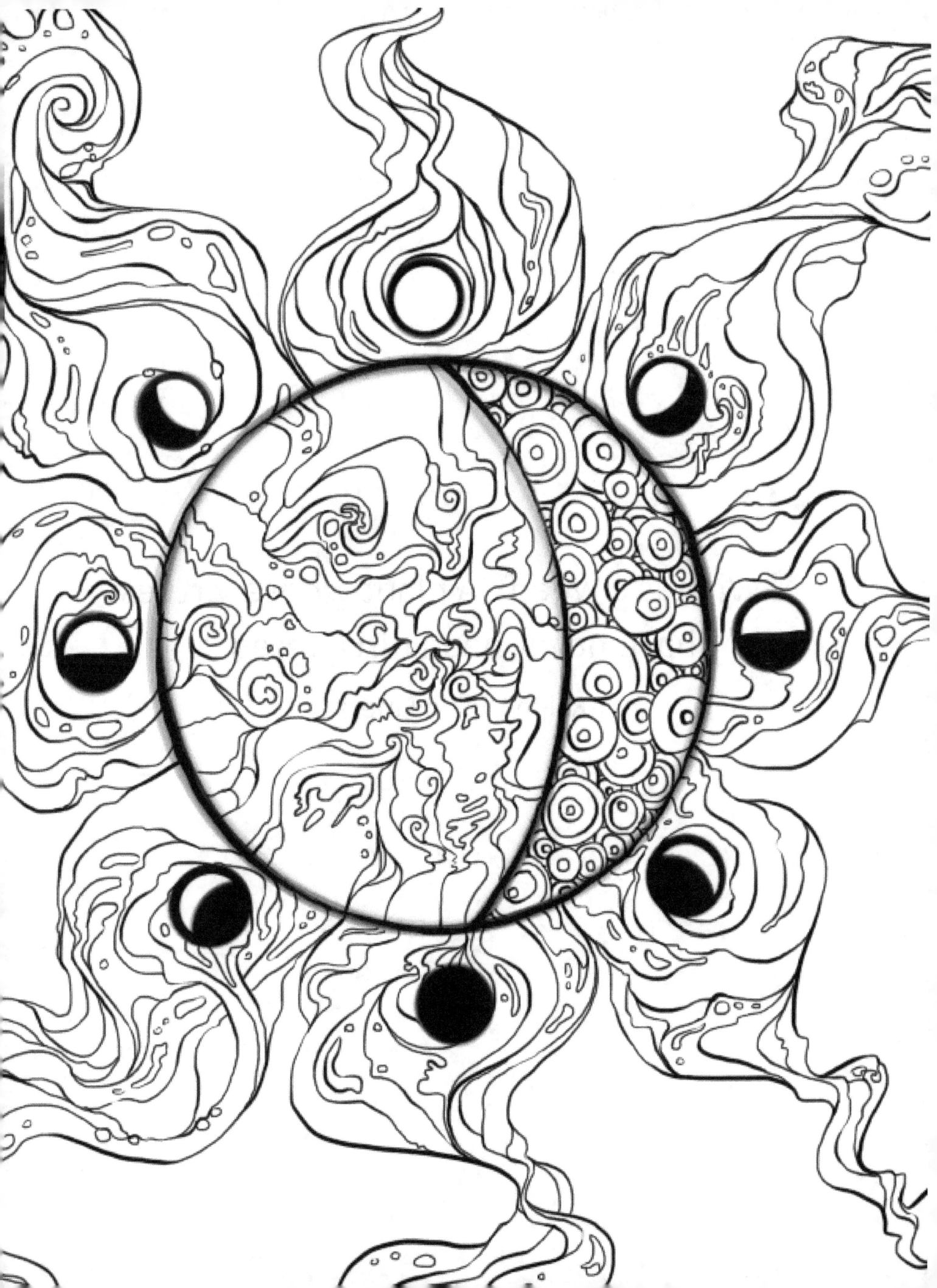

"What is a weed? A plant whose virtues have never been discovered."

-Ralph Waldo Emerson

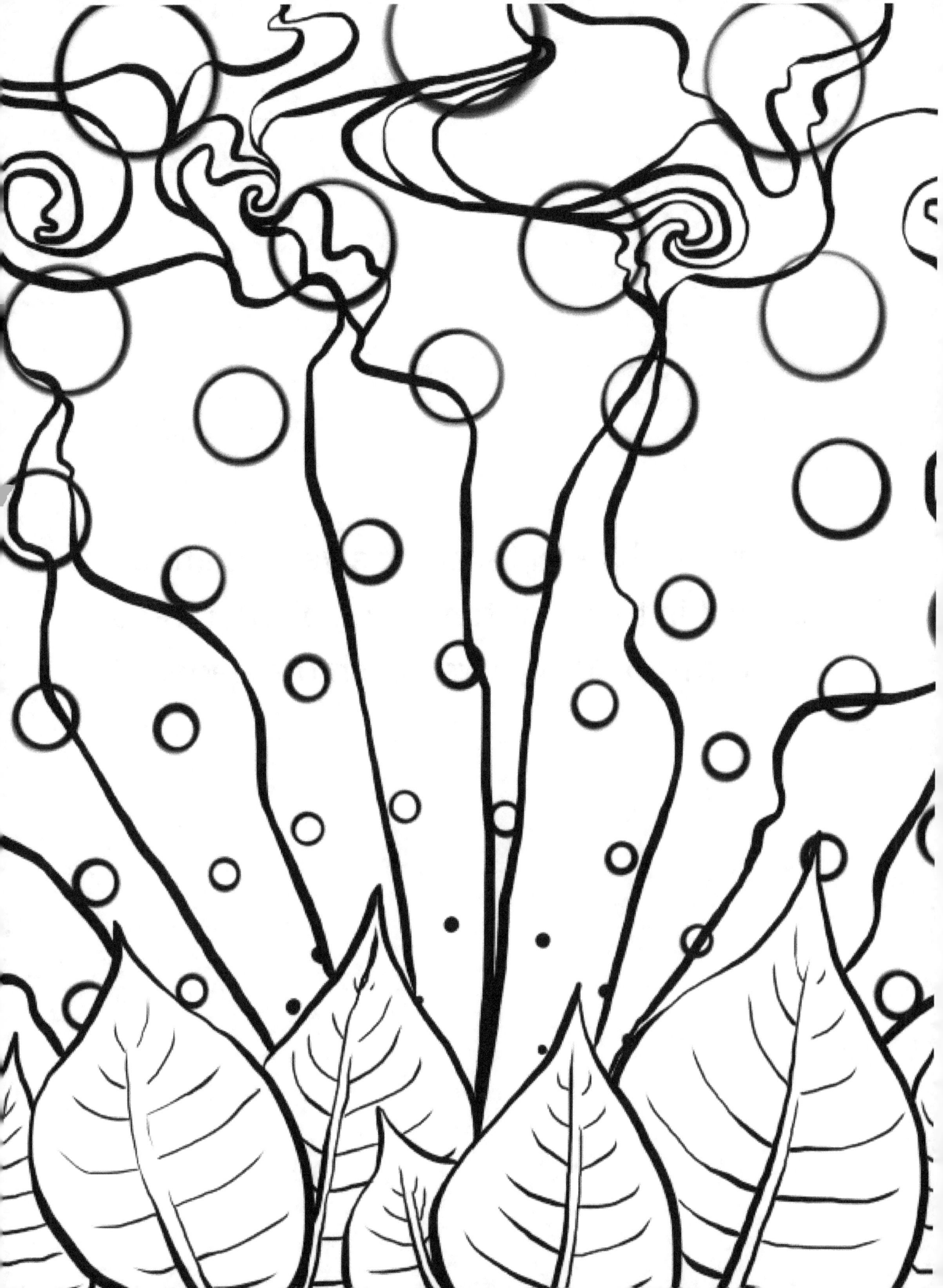

"If you think in terms of a year, plant a seed; if in terms of ten years, plant a tree; if in terms of 100 years, teach the people."

-Confucius

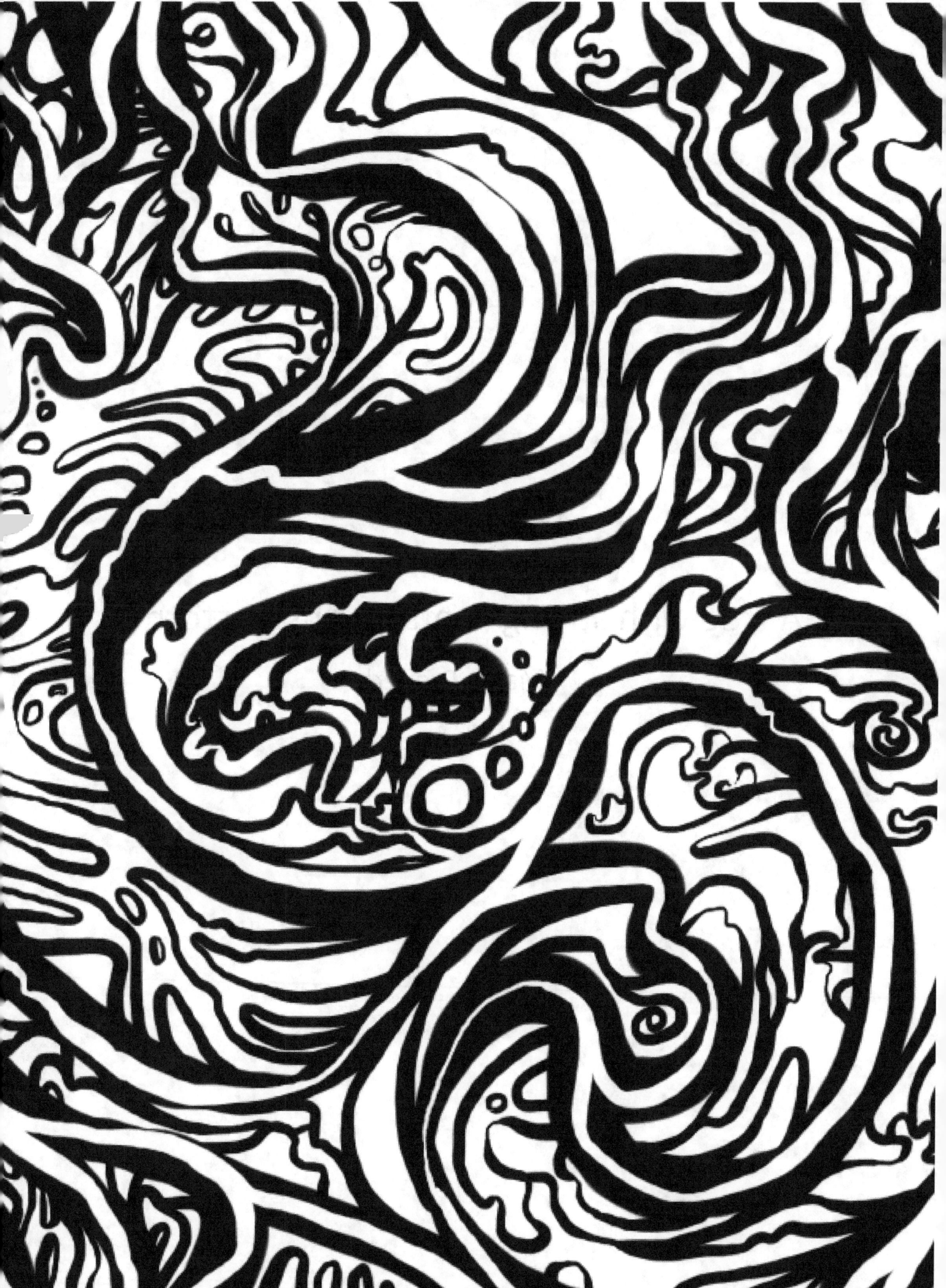

"A tree with strong roots laughs at storms."

-Malay Proverb

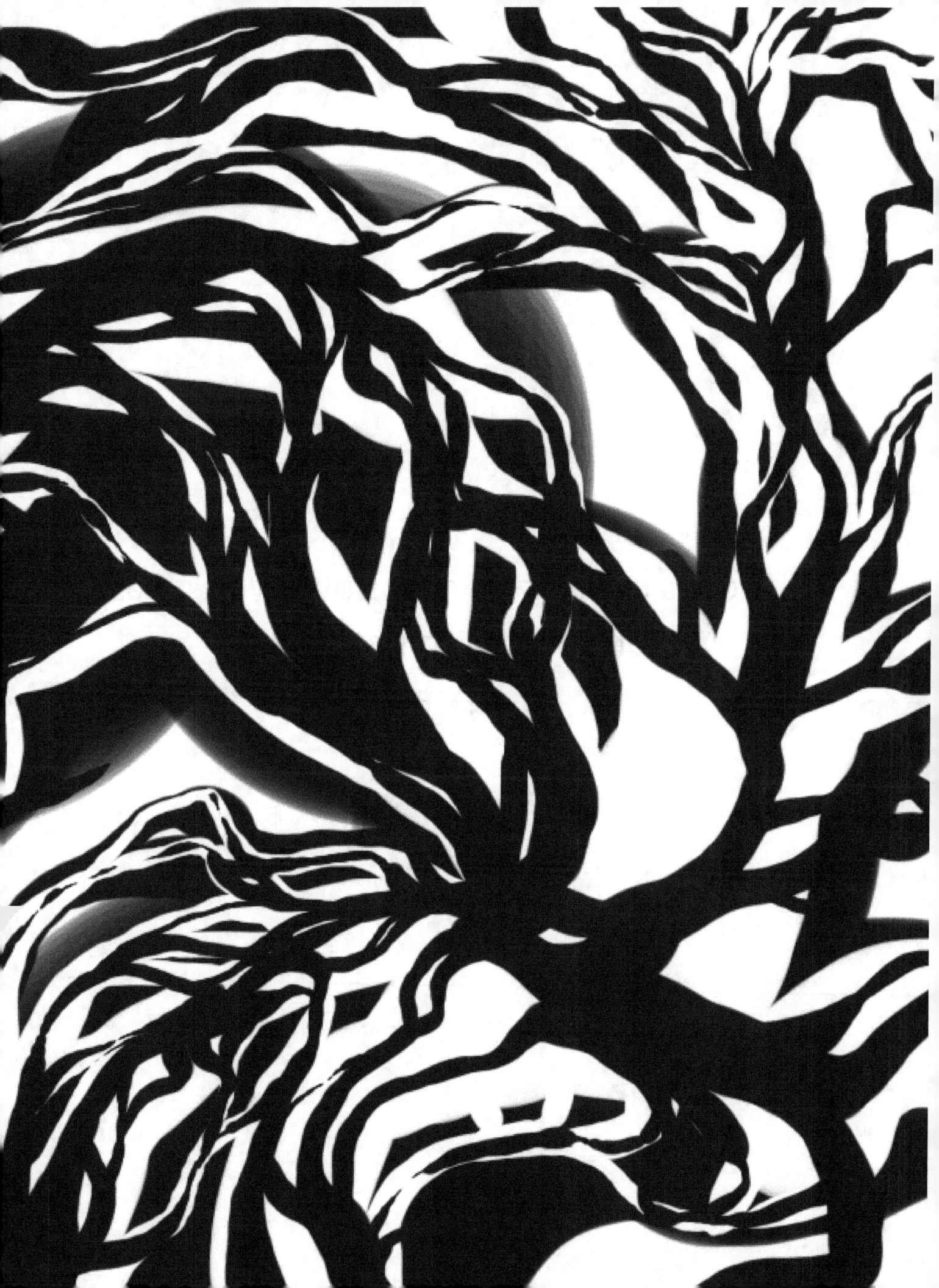

"It does not matter how slowly you go as long as you do not stop."

-Confucius

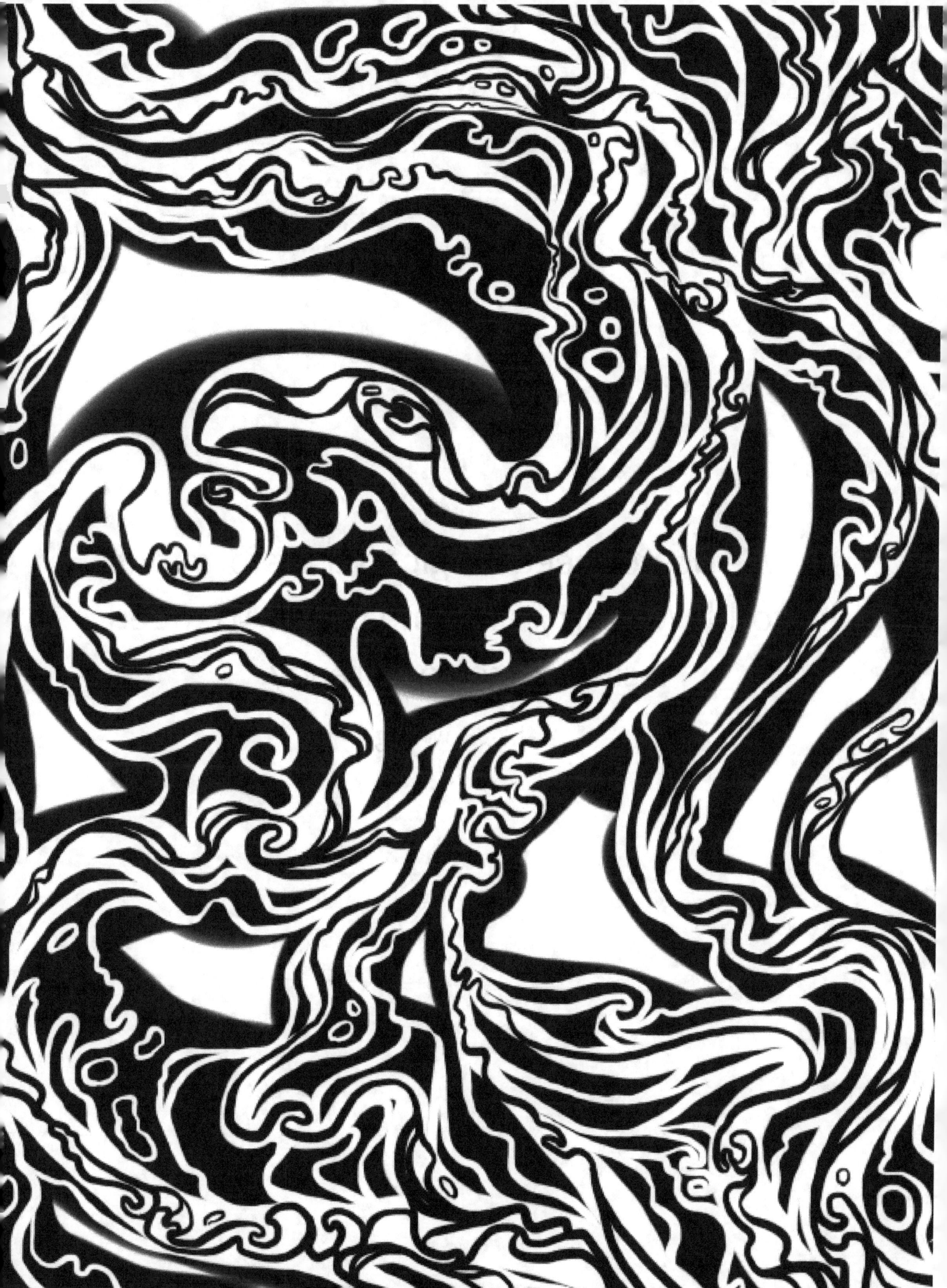

"We do not need magic to transform our world. We carry all of the power we need inside ourselves already."

-J.K. Rowling

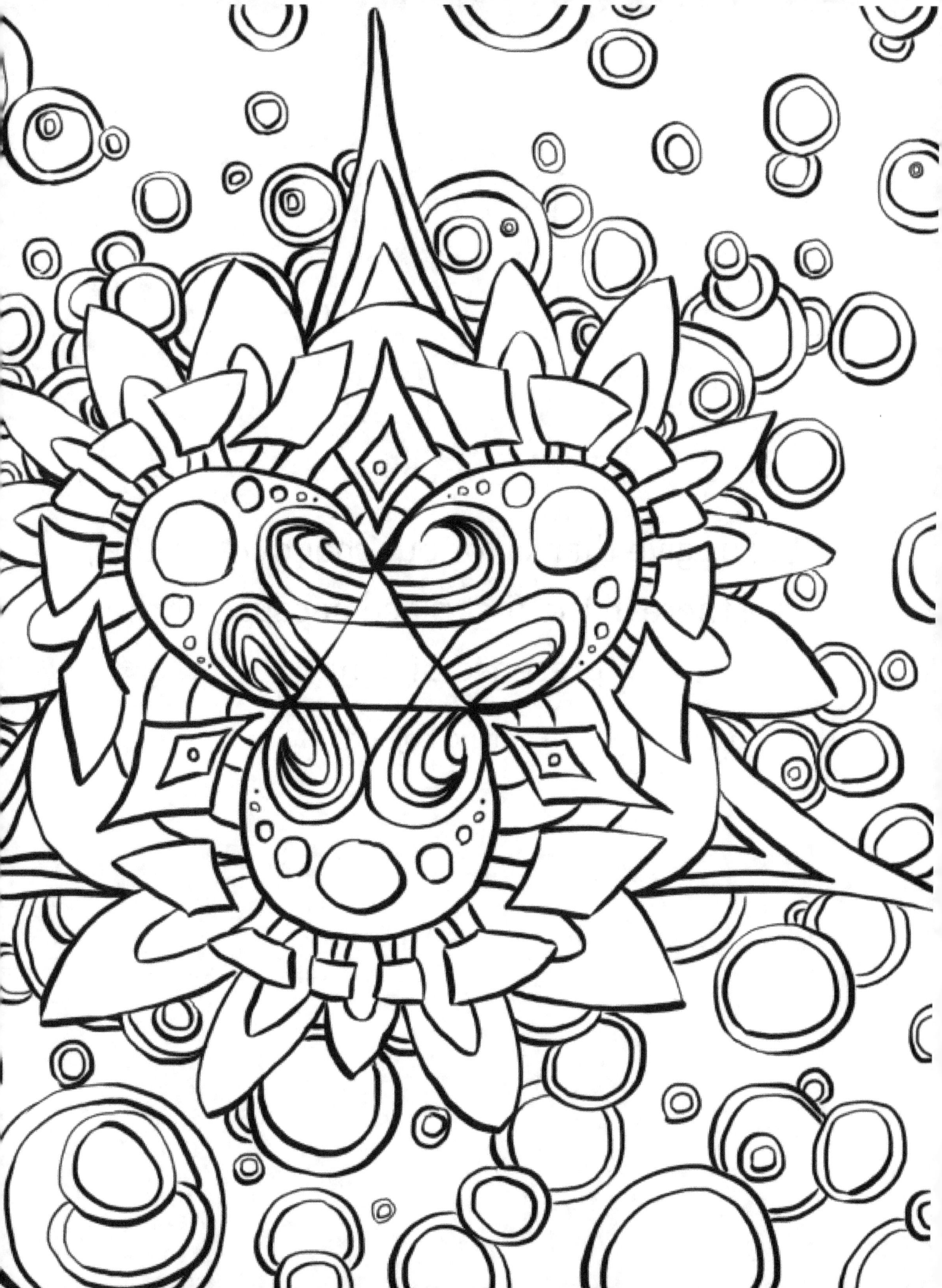

"Let us give thanks for our shadows for they are there in the first place because of the presence of light."

-Kamand Kojouri

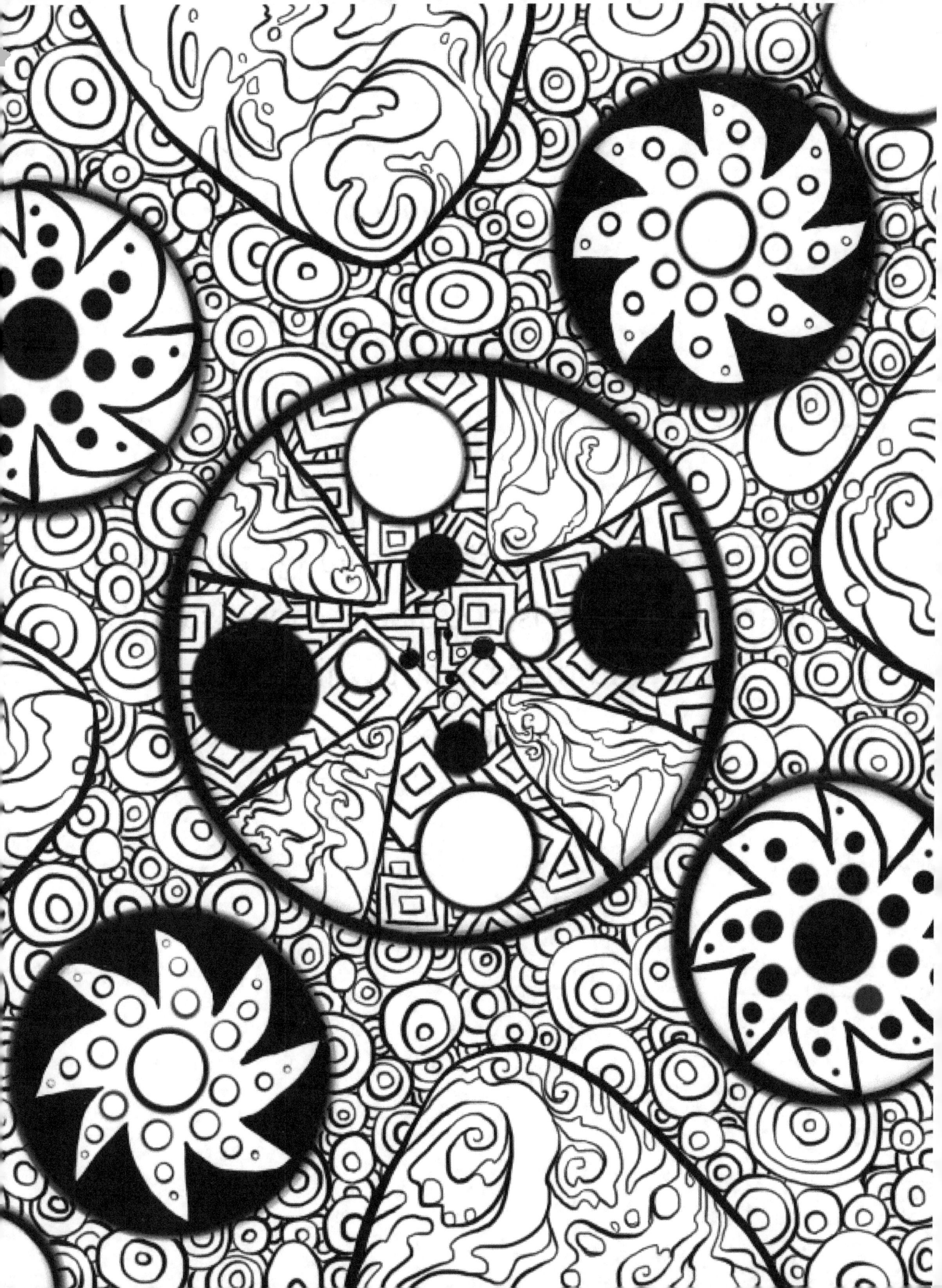

"There is yin and there is yang. There is black and there is not black. There is white and there is not white."

-Zen Koan

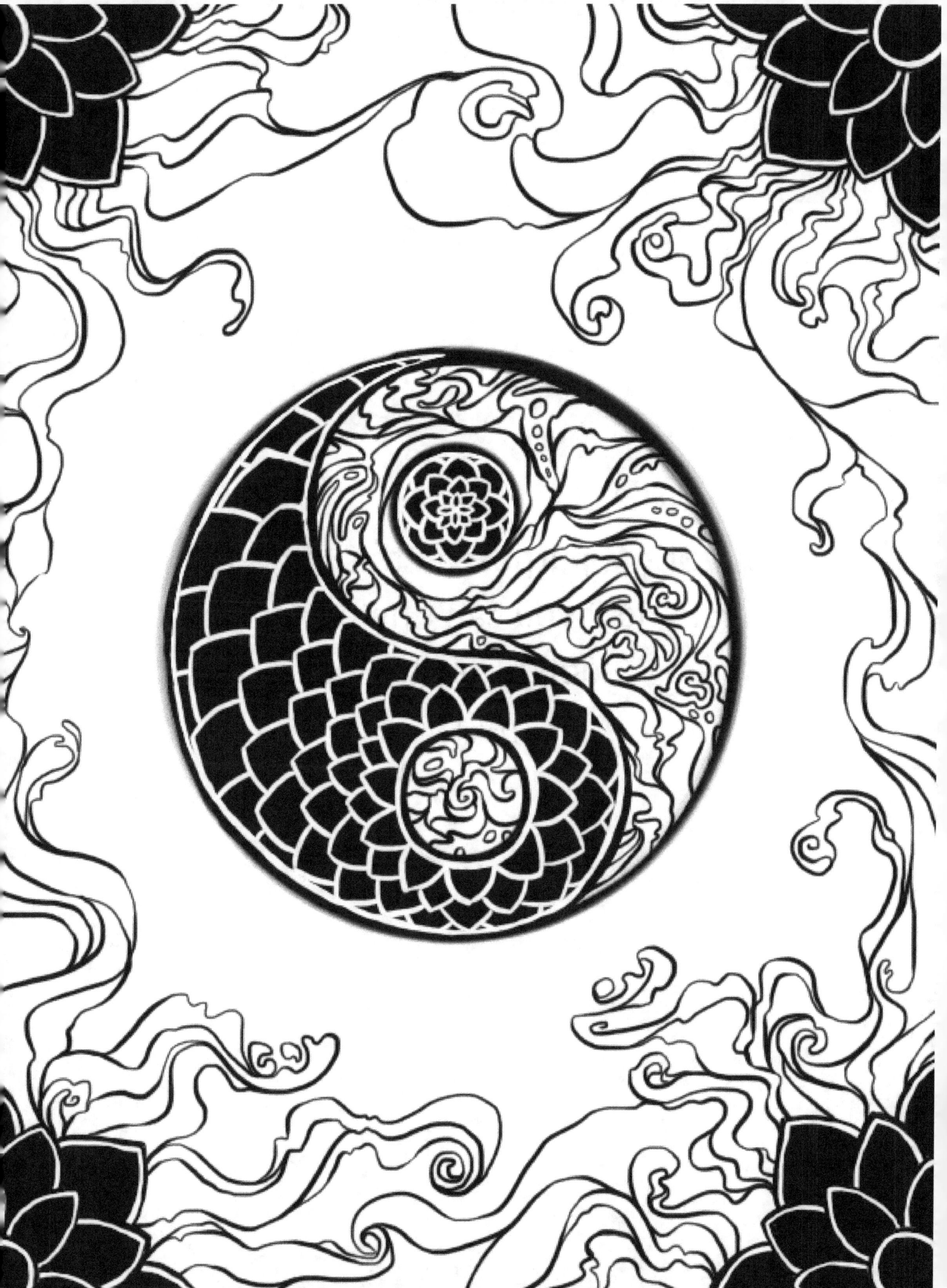

"Our prime purpose in this life is to help others. And if you can't help them, at least don't hurt them."

-Dalai Lama

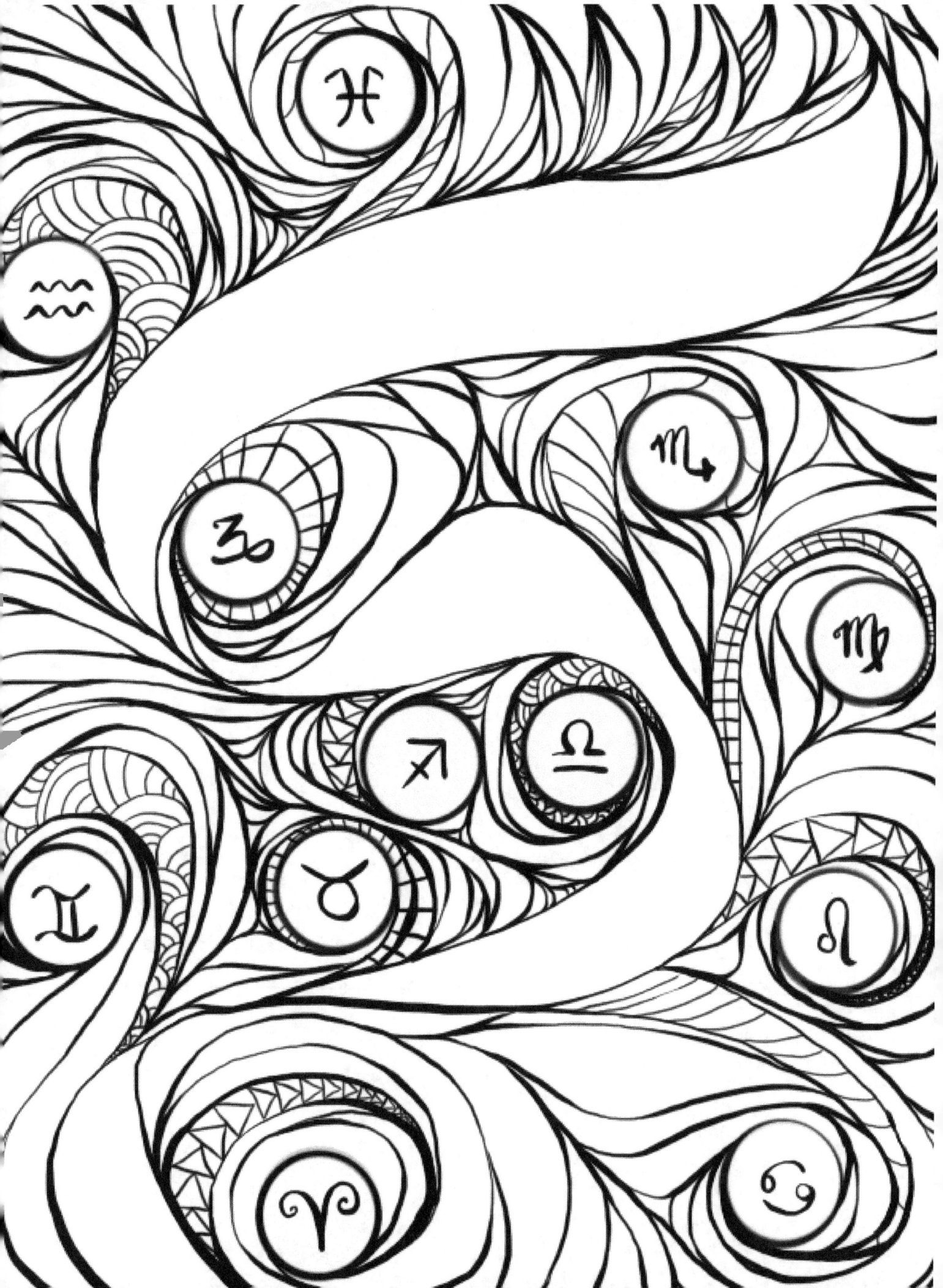

Thank you for being you!